an Isle of Wight

At the end of a rainbow . . .

HISTORICAL
Isle of Wight Pottery

Wheel-thrown
stripey pots
by Joe Lester,
Island Pottery Studio
Freshwater.

an Isle of Wight souvenir book

At the end of a rainbow . . .
HISTORICAL
Isle of Wight Pottery

Andrew & Lisa Dowden

First Edition 2006
ISBN 10: 0-9553616-0-5
ISBN 13: 978-0-9553616-0-9
© Andrew & Lisa Dowden 2006

Designed and written by Andrew & Lisa Dowden (based on
research by Lisa Dowden). Cover design Andrew Dowden.
Artwork/typesetting (in Technical and Arial) by Lisa Dowden.
Thanks to archaeologist David Tomalin
for information on ancient pots.

Photo credits:
Back cover, Steve
Wake LRPS. Unless
detailed with image,
all other photos
© Lisa Dowden.

All drawings
© Lisa Dowden.
(Reference maps
not to scale after
Bristow 1889.)

Published by
Buttercup Cottage Books
& Paper Products
PO Box 90
Sandown
PO36 6AP
T: 01983 867505

Printed by
The West Island Group Ltd
Afton Road, Freshwater
Isle of Wight PO40 9TT

British Library Cataloguing in Publication Data.
A catalogue record of this book is available from the British Library.

Contents

About this book

THIS ISLE OF WIGHT SOUVENIR BOOK – At the end of a rainbow ... Historical Isle of Wight Pottery – takes a brief look at wares made by eight historical Isle of Wight potteries admired and collected by Islanders, people across the Solent and further afield. It is by no means comprehensive, merely a snapshot of just a few of the pottery treasures you may encounter or, indeed, may already know about!

The book is intended to provide a quick and easy reference to some popular historical Isle of Wight makers, the aim being to raise public awareness of pottery made in the Isle of Wight. Colour illustrations, together with potters' marks, location maps, and brief details of each pottery are included. (For further in-depth reading of Island potters and potteries, see the recently published 'A Century of Ceramics' – details on page 47.)

For your information, we've also listed some Isle of Wight galleries, potters and museums you might like to visit (pages 44 to 46).

Please note that measurements are in centimetres – H. for height, W. for width, L. for length and D. for diameter.

We hope you enjoy reading about just a few of our Island's potters and potteries, and you never know, you may get hooked and want to seek out the others! Happy hunting!

Andrew & Lisa

At the end of a rainbow . . .
Historical highlights
& pottery today . . .

THE ISLE OF WIGHT is within close proximity to mainland England, yet to many its pottery appears to be lesser-known than that of a distant island cousin – Jersey. Surprisingly to some, makers in our beautiful 'Garden Isle' have been creating forms, mainly for domestic purposes, in 'burnt earth' for at least 5,000 years.

Pre-historic and Roman pots

The first pots found on the Island date to the Neolithic period (c4,000 to 2,000 BC), and ancient Islanders continued to make their wares throughout the Bronze Age (c2,000 to 750 BC) and Iron Age (c750 BC to AD43).

The Romans invaded the Isle of Wight in AD43 and brought with them new knowledge and skills. They produced a range of quite sophisticated pottery known as 'Vectis ware'. This varied in style and make-up but the black burnished Vectis ware produced, similar to wares made at Poole in Dorset at that time, are perhaps the best-known. When the Romans departed in the mid-4th century AD, so too did their expertise in making pots!

After the Romans –
pagan to medieval pots

The Anglo-Saxons produced unusual handmade pots, some adorned with applied knobs and impressed with home-made stamps. By the close of the first millennium the pots produced appear to be less adventurous.

A few pots from Norman times have been found to be made with particles of shell. Early medieval pots were decorated by thumb and finger. Glazed pottery was rare, but became more common in the 14th century.

Pottery from Dorset and Hampshire has been discovered on the Island dating from the post-medieval period. With pottery being brought in from across the Solent, it seems that the growth of our Island's potteries became restricted.

During the 19th century the Arts and Crafts movement revitalised the nation's interest in most things handmade. By the 20th century this permeated through to the Isle of Wight, heralding an awakening in the craft of pottery.

The early modern years

The Isle of Wight Handcraft Pottery, an offshoot of a brickworks in Gunville, used locally sourced clay to produce thrown domestic earthenware during the 1920s and 30s. Simple shapes, covered with high gloss and plain matt glazes, were decorated with linear designs, Art Deco patterns and, more rarely, studies of fruit, flowers and animals. The simple decorative designs were superseded

in the 1930s by an explosion of colour, with vibrant tur-
quoise, greens, pinks and blues fusing spontaneously in a
wash of running glazes.

The founder and owner of the pottery, Mr Samuel
Edgar Saunders, was not a potter. Residing at
Whippingham in East Cowes, Mr Saunders was a local
benefactor and prominent Island businessman with many
interests; his main profession revolved around the design
and development of boats and planes.

Reactive running
glazes of the Isle
of Wight Handcraft
Pottery.

Tallest H.20 cm

Mr Laye from Staffordshire was the first 'master' potter,
but by 1931 William Baker had taken over this role. He left
his father's pottery at Upchurch in Kent to start work at
Gunville where his dextrous throwing skills were employed.
Reginald Davies started at Gunville aged 17 in 1930. His
parents sighed relief when their son made good use of his
Cardiff Art School training to take up a post as principal
decorator at a pottery in the Isle of Wight, many miles
away from the Welsh coal mines. Manager and chief
glazer, Edward Jervison Bagley, joined the team in 1932.
He was an accomplished chemist and had many years'
experience at well-known potteries, such as the Ault and
Tooth factory and the Watcombe Pottery in Devon.

Bagley kept a secret recipe book, the contents of which, apparently, have never been seen by anyone! The reactive running glaze wares were highly successful during the 1930s, and Bagley's recipes are attributed to much of this success.

Early Isle of Wight Handcraft Pottery wares are often compared to Poole Pottery wares of the same period. This tenuous link has been investigated but to date no evidence has been found to connect the two.

Other early 20th-century Island potters include Ray Parsons and his wife Sybil (née Finnemore), of Yellowsands Pottery (latterly known as Bembridge Pottery), long associated with Bembridge School.

Ray and Sybil produced a broad range of mainly wheel-thrown functional and decorative items from the late 1920s to the mid-1960s, with only a break during World War II. These included mugs, bowls, jugs, lidded pots and lamp bases.

The image right shows one of the standard glazes and decorative techniques used by Ray and Sybil Parsons.

H.10 cm

Example of non-standard ware.
D.30.5 cm

Photo courtesy S Atwell

Typical Yellowsands Pottery
mark with Ray Parsons'
personal mark below.

Photo courtesy S Atwell

Enchanting sea horses and quirky fish

The Isle of Wight enjoyed a bonanza during the 1950s when sun-seekers, day-trippers and holiday-makers crowded onto ferries, trains and buses, and flooded into seaside towns.

Steaming locomotives pulled directly into Freshwater in the summer of 1953, where the Island Pottery Studio, founded by Joe Lester, flourished in the bustling environment.

Shelves were piled high beside the working potter at his wheel in the window. Vases, mugs and dishes, in all colours, shapes and sizes, adorned with cats, birds, fish, and enchanting sea horses, proved to be popular with tourists and are keenly sought after by collectors today.

The sunny 1950s swept into the swinging 60s with a whirlwind of change which continued into the 1970s. Isle of Wight pottery makers' wares also changed with the times, with stoneware and porcelain being more prominent, joining red and white earthenware pots in the show room.

African dream becomes a reality

Chessell Pottery near Yarmouth was founded by the late John Francis and his wife Sheila in 1978, following their return from Africa where they had taught and made ceramics for 14 years.

Created to harmonise with the natural world, their unique and individual range of purely decorative porcelain was based on water fountains, inspired by the magical coral gardens and swirling rock pools of the East-African coastline of Kenya. Sheila conceived and designed the complete range of handmade wares, so vast there are too many items to list here; from Wing, Cactus, and Poppy Seed Head vases in the 1970s, to successful Napkin Rings, the Moonflower range, Coral Reef Fish, and various water fountain designs, including unicorns and dolphins.

The fantasy animal figurine range included friendly, gentle Dragons. Mother Dragon launched the series in 1990 which was produced for over a decade and a favourite with members of the Collectors' Club. In 2001, John and Sheila decided to retire after almost 25 years of continuous successful trading at home and abroad. Production ceased in October 2002.

'New wave' ceramics

As in ancient times, 1980s and 90s ceramics echoed mainland trends and the individualism permeating throughout the UK ceramic scene. 'A Potter's Book', by Bernard Leach, inspired Molly Attrill to seek a potter's lifestyle. She set up her studio in 1982 in a 200 year-old barn, minutes away from the village of Newchurch.

Using red earthenware, Molly decorates her work using the methods of sgraffito and maiolica. Farm animals, including cockerels and pigs, creatures running wild, or images inspired by the surrounding sea, such as fish, lobsters and lighthouses, feature in her individual pieces.

Detail of a sgraffito design by Molly Attrill.

In 1996 Pauline Barnden fulfilled a lifetime ambition to set up her own Island studio. A fascination with the sea and geology, and a series of trial firings based on her own formulated glazes, resulted in a compilation of stunning pieces in hues of blue in the form of ammonites, sea shells, pebbles and stones.

Pauline has recently enlarged her range, and changed direction slightly by experimenting with paper-clay and flax to create delicate sea anemone forms.

She has now relocated to the West Country where she will continue to develop her ceramics.

Sea anemone in paperclay and flax by Pauline Barnden. Approx. D.20 cm

Photo courtesy Neil Barnden

Isle of Wight pottery today . . .

Islanders have always supported local artists and craftsmen; and pottery from decades past can be discovered by the keen collector at antique fairs, table-top sales and shows on the Island, and by browsing around curio shops. Island ceramists like Molly Attrill have regular customers to their studios throughout the seasons, as well as supplying work to Island and main-land galleries.

The Isle of Wight pottery scene today is buoyant with professional and upcoming makers relocating to the Island, such as Sue Paraskeva and Matthew Chambers; 'Cottage industry' potters like Cath and Ian Fletcher of Lodestone Pottery, quietly make their individual wares and sell through galleries.

Anyone interested in the ancient craft of ceramics can find examples at Island museums; and contemporary Isle of Wight ceramic makers' works are available either direct from the potters themselves, or via Island galleries and retail outlets. (See pages 44 to 46.)

Cath & Ian Fletcher of Lodestone Pottery produce stoneware inspired by nature.

H.20 cm

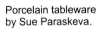

Porcelain tableware by Sue Paraskeva.

Photo courtesy Sue Paraskeva

Bembridge Pottery Studio

– Martyn Gilchrist
High Street, Bembridge
1965 to 1984

pottery mark – variations occur

MARTYN GILCHRIST worked for a year with Joe Lester in Freshwater before opening his own studio. Originally from Yorkshire, and in need of an occupation change, Martyn settled on the Island after visiting his parents here.

Various styles and methods were employed but Martyn's main distinctive wares incorporated wax-resist designs in stoneware. Many designs were by Coleen Donn (née Sharpe) who worked at the pottery for ten years as a principal decorator. Other designers included Annette Bonnet, who compiled a pattern book for the pottery (which also incorporated her own designs), and Krystyna Young's (of Haseley Manor Pottery) sister Barbara.

 Unusual pieces include all-over decorated, large stoneware pots; not very often seen chargers and costrels; and early earthenware pieces with quirky designs, as above.

Above Dog design by Annette Bonnet.
Collection of Mr D Morey
Photo courtesy Steve Wake LRPS

Stoneware pottery with wax-resist decoration made at
Bembridge Pottery Studio – Teapot, H.16 cm

Bristow Pottery
– Tony Bristow
Shore Road, Bonchurch – 1961 to c1967
Chine Hill, Shanklin – c1966 to 1972

pottery mark – variations occur

TONY BRISTOW set up his own pottery studio in Shore Road, Bonchurch, after many years practising pottery as a hobby.

He produced a variety of wheel-thrown and slip-cast domestic and ornamental wares. These included small pendants, bowls, vases, and goblets, along with many small animals that proved to be good sellers.

In the mid-1960s Tony opened a second studio in Shanklin, and pieces can be found with both Bonchurch and Shanklin marks made during this period. The Shanklin studio closed in 1972 when Tony moved to the USA to make pots there. Over the years he also had potteries in Malta, and Chillington in Devon. Tony's son Andrew set up his own studio, Bonchurch Pottery, in the Shore Road workshop in 1974. (See page 45 for contact details.)

Unusual pieces include any of the wide range of animals made during the 1960s, eg cats, frogs, lobsters – a set of three tortoises could be bought at the time for six shillings (30 pence); and large wheel-thrown decorated vases.

18

Cylinder with 'chattering' decoration.

H.13 cm

Right
Detail of chattering.
See page 42 for
definition.

Dragon vase
made *c*1966/67.

H.27.3 cm

Below
Decoration detail.

Chessell Pottery

– John & Sheila Francis A/ARCA
Brook Road, Chessell, Nr Yarmouth
May 1978 to October 2002

pottery mark from c1981 –
circular labels were also used

JOHN AND SHEILA FRANCIS A/ARCA returned to
England after 14 years teaching and making ceramics in
Africa, and converted a forlorn barn on a disused farm
into an industrious and highly successful pottery studio.

Purely decorative wares were made, based on water
gardens and the natural world. Initially stoneware pieces
were produced but very soon porcelain became the main
clay body used to create the delicate wares.

Each piece was unique being handmade, or cast and
hand-finished, and hand-decorated. Chessell Pottery
exported all over the world and its wares are highly
popular with collectors.

Unusual pieces include early stoneware and porcelain
designs; dinosaurs; Taurus the Bull; wares made for only
a short period, eg 'Ice Maiden' from the Decade range;
and limited edition Collectors' Club items.

Early wares produced at Chessell Pottery, with design ideas based on the natural world, included water gardens and seed pods. Stoneware pieces were made in the first few years, but by 1981 only porcelain was produced.

Wares were initially marked in black with a rubber stamp, superseded by an impressed 'cp' mark, on its own or with circular printed labels. Blue labels were used on early pieces followed by a white label, and latterly a clear label, all with either gold or silver lettering.

Centre piece – Poppy Seed Head in porcelain, H.9.5 cm

Fantasy animal figurines proved popular
with visitors and collectors alike.

Pegasus, introduced *c*1986
H.14 cm

John and Sheila Francis both enjoyed the
outdoor life, and horse riding was one of
their favourite pastimes.
Sheila's love of horses is apparent in her
attention to detail in the modelling of
this graceful creature.

Unicorn, H.17 cm

From top clockwise
An early porcelain
Shell Water Garden,
D.7 cm; Shell Water
Garden with
decorative glass in
base, D.9.5 cm;
Fern Shell
Water Garden, D.9 cm

Below
Tropical Fish
tallest H.10.5 cm

25

Haseley Manor Pottery

– Krystyna Young
Haseley Manor, Arreton
1976 to 2000

pottery mark – variations occur

HASELEY MANOR POTTERY was set up by Krystyna Young and her husband Raymond, at their home Haseley Manor. Krystyna ran the pottery while Raymond concentrated on the house. Both became major tourist attractions, with proceeds from the pottery contributing towards restoration and upkeep of the historic building.

A stylised flower is the main decorative feature of Haseley Manor Pottery wares; a design which echoes the artistry of Krystyna's and her sisters', Barbara and Yolanda (who also worked at the pottery), Polish ancestry. Pieces were made to 'mix and match' in red earthenware, using in-house coloured slips to decorate.

Sadly Krystyna passed away in 1988 but her creativity continued in the wares produced at Haseley Manor Pottery until its closure in September 2000.

Unusual pieces include large, all-over decorated jugs and bowls; tea and coffee sets; and non-standard commissioned items.

Commissioned ware.
Goblets, H.15 cm

Jug, H.15 cm

Island Pottery Studio

– Joe Lester

Station Road (School Green Road) & Avenue Road
Freshwater, 1953 to c1978

pottery mark – variations occur

JOE LESTER relocated his pottery studio from a shed in his garden, to a shop in Station Road with a double-bay window. The pottery subsequently moved to Avenue Road and later back again to School Green Road (formerly Station Road).

The brightly-coloured white earthenware pieces, often decorated with rainbow banding and enchanting sea horses, were greatly favoured by tourists.

Joe Lester's son Joseph took over the pottery in the late 1970s, and went on to establish his own studios at Alum Bay, and then at Yarmouth with his daughter Renella. In 1993 she set up a studio on her own in Yarmouth and ceased trading in 2001.

Unusual pieces include early abstract decorated pots, and pots with running glazes; large pieces with all-over decorated designs; and sgraffito wares, particularly with animal subjects.